NAVEL STRING

For Lettie

ADRIAN AUGIER

NAVEL STRING

PEEPAL TREE

First published in Great Britain in 2012
Peepal Tree Press Ltd
17 King's Avenue
Leeds LS6 1QS
UK

ISBN 13: 9781845232023

Supported using public funding by
ARTS COUNCIL
ENGLAND

CONTENTS

SEAFARERS

The new gull signs the opening sky
in the name of the Father and the coming sun

and the foreday mornin' fisherman,
one wiry form uncoiling

from the unlit crevice of Conway
from the charcoal crotch

of Foux-a-Chaud,
the yawning underarm of Trou Ganier.

This first is always
Peter, full of faith,

who walks in grace with God,
who haunts the gaunt half-light,

who, defying the advance of age,
gives thanks for this day

where the chill is slight
and grits in only half his joints

rusting slowly by the sea
he wants to ride each day.

Mesi Bondiay, he can still face
his fierce and fickle ocean,

this couldn't-care-less lover
who teases him

and his seafaring brothers
with her deep blue treachery,

rattling their mortality
with foretastes of death and heaven too –

white cotton angel wings
of nothing more

than their own bleached shirts
dovetailed against her frocking blue,

mocking their faithful names
Ol' Peter, Tall-boy John,

Mathew-Macko
and Simon…

which other name for Simon
both God and I forget.

Despite the jeer and threat
and flying spittle

off the winded surf,
these water-borne apostles

ascend on waves taller than
trees which beget canoes

and this adventuring Peter,
captain of a craft dug out

from the wooden heart of centuries,
without benefit of chain

or flag or cannon fire, reclaims
for God as much as for himself

all that island kingdom he has seen
crowning what by now must surely be his sea.

And when against a dusking sky
he hitches up his skirted nets,

asking Father and reclining sun
for some omen he can borrow,

that same Peter divines
good fortune in a trinity of gulls

drawing the horizon's thread
along the edge of sea and sky,

homing him to patchwork hills;
home, mostly because

is there he born and there
he will surrender his last sigh

amid the twine of hillside roads
with their tangle of familiar names:

Morne du Don, Pavee,
Old Calv'ry, La Pansée.

But for now,
Ol' Peter dowses lantern light

to walk with God
into bright sea-water dreams

laced tight with trust
and just a little rum,

his cup of years crusted with salt,
and slowly rusting expectation,

still hopeful, despite the hour,
for a few good days

and the eventual redemption,
here or in the next,

of which all heart and head has dreamt
and to which he will be remembered

in the omen of the early gull,
at the flowering of half-light

before the opening eye of day,
if fate and God permit

Ah oui, si Bondiay vlay.

JABAL

for the island muse to whom our craft is moored

We met secretly at first
in a dim-lit bower, by an estuary,
amid the blacklace of breadfruit shadow
quilting bits of fallen sky,
making afternoon a sanctuary
for tasting air and love and light.

But now, more common than before,
we find her in the street,
shutters open to her soul,
the eye of an aggressive sun
burning through thin layers
of her inexpensive modesty.

We were her first transgression,
her initial compromise.
We knew the incongruity,
her first uneasy pain,
that slow thrust of steel
into the soft brown heart.

We felt the withheld breath
the rhythmic moan
the awkward turning of a town
becoming vulgar
flirting with fluorescent style.
Then came others

bargaining beneath a buzz
of street lights,
making easy coinage
to the music of loose change,
banking on the currency
of our earlier corruption.

And still, she stole our breath,
caught our eye, hid our sighs
in folds of water-blue dwiettes,
suspended disbelief in a pearl of full-moon,
a swirl of studded sea-shawl,
a brooch of diamante sun.

And, as we gasped incredulous for air,
she would turn a flourish of her seasons,
persuade us with some perfect fruit
of her most casual labour,
allow some secret indiscretion
in the bosom of her hills.

But in her bold new world
she has sold
the shade beneath
her parasols of palms,
let out her gold ribbons
by the shore,

pawned the sun-set brooch,
forsaken lanterns of k-oil,
her lamp-la-vierge
with its holy tongue of fire.
And her magic,
once only imagined

behind the blades of jalousies,
beyond wood-gated balconies,
is now arrayed
as vendors' trays
on Chausée sidewalks, laid out
along insomniac Marchand.

Her virtue spent in some watering hole
or hillside haunt, we hear her
shuffling home before the dawn
humming a lacomette,
some l'histoire of unlasting love
unlamented lives and small farewells

left better unperformed,
as in early morning light
she unhurriedly unstraps,
unlaces and unties the bonds
which are our tender moorings
to her shore.

UNDER HEAVEN
for Robert

Though each of a thousand wagging leaves
vainly proclaims its own green tongue
when moved they make
one chorus under heaven.

Mouben, maho, mahogani, mango,
each for its sacred reason
will blossom, fruit or branch or bud,
according to its season.

Though rivers crave serpentine ways
and circumvent the stony will,
sweet, salt or brackish brine
they are His waters, still.

If instead we owned these days
no conceit of ours would sustain
the hosanna of each sunrise, the gloria
of waves, baptisms of warm rain.

But look upon the sea's diurnal labour,
her selfless ritual repeating,
now departure, now return,
tendering and retreating,

washing feet at high brown cliffs
where pebbles make their humble offering,
where devoted waves draw breath
before their fervent proffering.

She churns the stony multitudes to chanting
incantations which no heart ignores,
there, under gazing white-winged gulls
beneath the spell of frigates shadowing the shore.

And at the reeféd altar of the evening
the brazen wave relinquishes its crown;
each tide erases a transgression, bids
the ocean lay its bleachéd banners down

there in faith to kneel, and await
the promised light which will forgive all wrongs,
even the dead bark which once was
a babel of green tongues.

Days, waters, mountains, leaves;
if it were not for men, I might believe.

IT'S A HARD THING

It's a hard thing
to live without passion
in a place that is part of you
to stay all level-headed
when you feel
the wind like it's
your own hot breath.

It's a hard thing

when you know a place so well
that you can tell from the smell
inside the damp wood house
and the dark drumming on the zinc roof
that August rain falling heavy like a rake
and ripping 'way your skin
from the very surface of the earth.

It's a hard thing

when in dry season
you see all the soil crack-up
like a big brown heart that split apart
and all the happiness that come
from loving green leaf
and bubbling spring
done gone and evaporate into air.

It's a hard thing

to stay all cool and comfortable
and smile for people who you know
would fuckup a place that is your home
since before you born,

because three generations before you
struggle, struggle, struggle
till they buy a house

and land, together,
and get to own the place
that their great-grandfather
used to rent
but could never buy
in his one life
before he die.

It's a hard thing

not to cry, when this place is part of you
as much as the hand that hold the pen
to write this thing, that same pen
that your godfather give you
when you pass for college,
that pen with its deep dark ink
that flow like a bloodline from it.

It's a hard thing

and you would know
because there must be a dose
of shame or pain or something else
inside you there, beside this craving
for a longtime day
when we used to understand
that history is not what people tell us

but part of who we are:
deep-thinking people
who still want to tell our story
under moonlit mango tree

or street lamp, in painting, or in poetry
or in that sweeter music which used to come
bubbling-up from deep inside a place

where we were not, like now, afraid to go.
Because we owe a debt, a loyalty
to this landscape that sustain us,
this earth that raise you, raise me,
that should make us ask ancestors
if it is alright to cut down a tree
that is older than we,

because somebody navel string
might be buried under there.

THE HARRIED NIGHT

So let the harried night forget.
Let it sing its jaded chorus

to the tarnished chalice of the sun,
its lancing beam

inciting bougainvillea
to thrust its prickled tongue

at morning's drizzle.
Let the brazen croton

imitate hell's ire
and if noon's noxious fumes ignite,

well, we had been warned
the end would come by fire.

PERHAPS THE CHILDREN

Worry, but don't panic yet.
It's just a theory

that perhaps the children
don't need our poetry,

as citizens of this one great world
don't need the baggage of identity.

We have raised them well,
to be content, not knowing what is lost,

not knowing why we have surrendered
or what assimilation costs.

We too will soon have forgotten;
first the words and then the images dissolve.

But perhaps, this global generation
does not need to know our battles,

has no vexing issues to resolve,
only to work the nine to five

and learn to love the fading light,
and drink and drive and live

all week to blow each Friday night.
And if we ourselves are not quite sure

then let them at least wine down
the weekend fête;

no need to sober and speak out;
no urgency to wake them yet.

Incidentally, last week three schools
and a church were vandalized,

and the "wise" among us still expect
society by some miracle to rationalize

that there can be no funds for luxuries
like theatres and libraries –

certainly not before
the madhouse is completed.

No national discussion
just loud positions, unsuitably informed.

No parliamentary debate meanwhile,
no eloquence to inspire or even to beguile.

Only the banality
of little men laid bare:

a lot of craft
but scarcely any art out there.

We find anarchy of course,
the type that titillates the streets

sets head against heart,
ego against ego,

the blade against the gun,
but still admit no blame, no reason

for the aberrations we feel
our children will become

without the wonderment of words,
the careful turning of a phrase,

the subtlety of tone and texture
that once raised our letters, songs and sermons

beyond the one-dimensional:
so brave, defiant, unconventional.

On this soil
there must not be a drought of poets,

even though some grow old and tired
crisscrossing the same crumbling bridge

of words. Worry, but don't panic, yet.
It's just a theory

that perhaps the children really
just don't need our poetry.

IN THE PARENTHESIS
for D.W.

In the parenthesis
after a brother's eulogy
he images his final syllables:
ink stains on a watercolour sky,

the late light bleeding
shore into charcoal sea,
releasing slow
dissolving cumuli.

He lingers there,
suspended in mid-metre,
wishing for a brush of rain
to wash the dimming monochrome,

hoping that a tear might weigh
as much as an overdue confession,
that one true verse as much as any prayer
will see a brother's spirit safely home.

Once, this island,
shedding pretence,
posed eager for his pen,
impatient for his palette,

and together in a moment
they had witnessed
morning glory shining like a promise
from behind her silhouette.

But not now,
not in this void
bracketed by dusk
and dividing death;

not in this parenthesis
with its encumbrances
of broken halves and
unbrothered flesh.

LANDFALL

It was easy to believe
the thrill of landfall
would not wane,
would ever sail us on,
the high of mountain spines
always send blood racing
like ground lizards
tremoring
the brown earth
underskin.

Easy to accept sincerity
from unbroken bays,
unblemished estuaries
where only gods
had entered,
and still adventure
under shade of guardian palms
in the arms of bois-canou,
in shrines of golden light
and evergreen bamboo.

But such idle dreams implode;
perspective shatters
on the road to reason;
pundits read the signs of sin
and scorn and anarchy and treason.
Others look to heaven,
scouring the night for stars,
or raise their torch
to scorch the darkness
with their fire.

Most are eager
only to be first
to sight and claim
the greening promise
of a young empire.
Fewer think
a windblown seed,
despite its prodigal digressions,
will sink eventually down
and find good earth,

and, fathering a forest
of conviction,
a second birth,
will send a rush
of new blood
racing
like ground lizards
tremoring
the brown earth
underskin.

DRY WINDS AT EASTER

for Florence La Guerre and her daughters

Dry winds at Easter
whisper old spirituals
shuffling soles of wry leaves
as they dance the parched earth
under her bedroom window

Come go to glory

Dry winds of Easter
tilt the spire of a proud palm,
a green moment
in the picture frame
of her small window on the sky

Come go to glory with me

Dry winds at Easter
rustle the parchment
of light-filled days,
reassuring her with their return
that they have not forgotten her singing

Come go to glory with me,
bye-bye, bye-bye, mi Lord.

Yet another season
touches the boughs of the old julie mango,
old even when she was young,
not so long ago, before she married
into this plateau of possibilities.

Can you hear those angels singing
bye-bye, bye-bye mi Lord,
hear those angels, singing...

Dry winds of Easter
tease the furrowed bark
of the brittle red plum tree,
wanting another flock of green
to alight on its limbs,

and that audacious avocado
that never bore
until the year she swore
and threatened it:
Bye-bye, bye-bye, mi Lord!

We gonna walk and talk with Jesus,
bye-bye, bye-bye, mi Lord,
walk and talk with Jesus,
bye-bye, bye-bye, mi Lord

Glory Alleluya, yes my Lord,
Glory Alleluya…

Her memory touched the trees
growing slowly
just beyond her window,
growing slowly like her three children,
whom she knew no one would mind –

not their father.
His eyes had not met hers
since the sickness stole her light,
stole her right
then her left breast.

Like the trees
her children
would find strength
as she had done,
from within.

They would find strength
from the soil that they were planted in.
That was her legacy.
Yes, Lord,
that was her bequest!

Gloria lay lu ya.
Yes, my Lord!
Glo ri a lay lu ya.

Eyes closing,
she could still see
beyond the frame of jalousie doors
and the exes of verandah rails,
the Easter lilies.

They rose again every year,
their wide smiles
urging her on:

Come go, come
go to glory with me;

their white cluster
like an oasis
in the shadowed yard
she hoped again to cross,
closing the distance,

closing the distance
between the bed
that claimed the body
and the voice
that called her soul

to seek
the deep
green groves
of bamboo in the back yard
beyond the ravine…

She smiled behind her tired lids
the white window in her mind
easing her pain,
firing her heart,
beckoning her

through the old wood walls
under the call
of the dry Easter wind
that only she could hear,
and the old stream

under the green groves of bamboo
and the clasp of ferns
and the crisp watergrass
where the soil always wept
and yielded softly underfoot

We gonna walk and talk with Jesus,
bye-bye, bye-bye mi Lord,
walk and talk with Jesus

And only she could understand
the cool murmur of the stream
that had come from the mountain
to take her hand, to take her home,
chanting her soft to heaven,

Come go to glory with me,
come go to heaven
with me, come go…

even now, under the dry wind,
she did not want to wait.

She had chosen her shroud
which Da' had made
at night in her back room,
warm, grey partition walls
muraled with magazine faces smiling back.

In the dancing light of her lamp
Da' sewed as only a woman for a woman can,
with those angels singing:
Come go, come go to glory, with me...
Yes, my Lord?

Her husband
should have made the casket
as she had asked two days ago
when first she heard
the dry Easter wind

coming over those hills,
calling the rains, calling to her
and the stream of her childhood.
He should have known
she did not want to wait,

should have understood
this once, this once, O' Lord,
bye-bye, bye-bye mi lord.
Going up to heaven...?
Yes my Lord.

Gloria lay lu ya
Yea, smile Lord...
Gloria lay lu u ya

WITHOUT THE WEIGHT OF CEREMONY

for Sabby who remains unfound

Without the weight
of ceremony or loud repentance,

we who have inherited
this devastated world

begin old rituals of acceptance,
plumbing the depth of our endurance,

despite the threat and curse and blessing
of more rain. We place again our faith

where it will thrive beside the planted seed,
hiding our hope inside a whispered prayer.

We make our peace with an unscripted future,
draw solace from the dribble of a stream,

and, smoothing the creases from our memories,
freshen the faces of our kin,

and, when we are spent, alone
and longing for reunion, we divest

our losses in a sigh and await
the kindnesses, the late rites of communion,

which we know must surely come
before faith fades or expectation ends:

blessings from the hearts of far-flung family
and the healing hands of old well-wishing friends.

DID I NOT LIFT MINE EYES

Did I not lift mine eyes
unto the hills
above the city cracks,
high above the vanity
of their mirror-glass and steel

beyond this viral pox of roofs
the turning tar
the hellish smell of burning rubber
the ceaseless trafficking
in restlessness?

Did I not hold firm
in the heated breath
of their brewing storms
and pray to you
through all temptation,

through their attempted shroudings
of the seeing eye of sun,
through eclipses of the blood-red moon,
forsaking idolatry
and denouncing evil doers?

Did I not kneel
before this green almond sea
and praise your hand
whose sculpting made us
from earth and spittle

pain and power
proud and handsome as this land?
And did you not see
my raiséd eyes
full of fire,

eternal righteousness
and indignant scorn
fit to be unleashed
upon the house of fools?
Was I too wicked

to want them dead?
Did you not also
envisage them gone
from the grace
of this green earth,

their haggling
in our temples ceased,
their revelry by our waters cursed,
the defiling of our children
turned upon their kin,

the corruption
of our soil undone,
the cold white of their eyes put out…?
And did I not hold my tongue
and wait

for your hot wrath
to kindle brimstone
in their halls
so that they would leave our land
and not return to us?

Lord, you know all,
not I,
who can only look
upon your hills,
but if not from you,

and soon,
then whence,
how,
and why not now,
cometh our help?

INHERITANCE
for Lettie

Perhaps it is your way,
this wordless waiting
on the fractured island
of your cracked front step,
eyes locked tight against the sun
so that the world turns prematurely red
behind uneasy lids
thinning with veiled dread
of passing uninherited.

Perhaps it is your way,
listening soundless for alarm
under the fearless frolic
of grandchildren
gushing in the distance down
by the rushing yard-pipe,
flaying brown, brittle limbs
in short-lived spontaneity.

Perhaps this is your way,
this wise unspeaking pause
tuning out the tele-radio
selling guile, the pretensions
of vote-mongers
peddling promises
of nothing
but their own perpetuity.

Perhaps it is your way,
this silent resistance
this patient peacelessness
defying the ignorance
that has become our circumstance

threatening to leave us
undescribed and disinherited
behind closed lids
when the world turns red.

LISTEN TO THE DARK YOUNG MEN

Listen to the dark young men;
they laugh in waves
too loud to mask the terror
in their heaving chests,
tight skin holding in mistrust,
tensioned muscles
muffling the tremor
of an earthquake.
Like magma brooding
just below a crust,
they wait
for some mirror-smoke messiah
to march them to a willing edge
to help them fly to heaven
in a pledge of faith.

They could leap
and leave behind
the servitude,
the persistent poverty,
or, just as easily,
they could stay
and any day
set aflame
the city.

DUNCAN DE LA CROIX

My God,
when I in awesome wonder
consider all the worlds thy hands have made...

Still, Duncan's death
draws me back,
back to crossroads at La Croix,
back through the threat of rain
weaving a grey canopy
for his mourning village,

dull pain of thunderings
in sky and head
and soul.

I hear the rolling thunder,
thy power throughout the universe displayed...

We shuffle remembering why
remorse returns
always too soon,
why this black belt of bitumen
pauses for a memory here
but never stops.

Never stops, O Lord,
except at churched doors
except like now, for Duncan.

Then sings my soul, my saviour god
to thee, how great thou art!
How great...

In a seedy corner lot
a rubbled wall
reads like a gravestone
where Acam's house
had bravely stood, before the fire
sent her to a sister in New York —

Acam's proud home, where we once sipped
sweet milky Sunday-mornings
from the warm belly
of her flowered teapot,
taken down on special days
from a treasury of shelved porcelain.

> *And when I think that God, his son not sparing,*
> *sent him to die, I scarce can take it in*

In the back street
Ma Lamoire's quiet house-front
still hides its secrets
behind dust-brown jalousies,
nailed now, shut from prying eyes
since her lonely silent passing.

> *Now sings her soul O Saviour God to thee*

Surely, there is more here than waiting death!
Others join the shuffle upwards, always
to the old-stone church where prayers
congregate with song and incense.
They step out of chattled lives,
white funeral shoes in hand;
they come from the hills in hats.

> *Then sings my soul*

From their humble homes
and rusting rumshackles
hugging this ragged coast
they come praying softly
for ascensions of the faithful,
they come singing

       My Saviour God to Thee.

They come to speak farewells, and fondly
to remember him despite his sins
beneath death's threatening sky.
They come, my Lord,
to lay him with the faithful departed
to lay him in your peace.

       Then sings my soul,
       my Saviour God, to thee

No less, they come to see the living,
to see Elvis, down from Brooklyn,
and if his money shows,
how far it goes
before the wake runs dry;
to see what Helen bring from England

for her cripple child,
the mirror image she scarce remembers
except at times like these;
to see Winsburt who made good in Texas
and Pricillia come from St. Christ
with her white man;

       Now sings her soul!

and relatives and friends
choke momentarily
on recollections.

> *My Saviour God to thee...*

Pots gurgle familiar fragrances
in the yard below, and on the widow's stove,
attended by godmothers singing softly,

> *How great Thou art, how great...*

Old school friends
and fellow fishermen assemble
and white rum flows like tears,

> *When Christ shall come with shouts of acclamation*
> *and take me home, what joy shall fill my heart...*

before the drums and conches
and his braying dog at dusk
send him through this first of nights,

> *Then shall I bow in humble adoration*
> *and there proclaim my God, how great Thou art...*

this night to which we all must come
despite our vanity.

> *My Saviour God, to Thee.*

Our sympathies conveyed, we leave
quietly; before the storm, we say politely,
retreating to our own sanctuaries,

How great Thou art
How great...

crossing the flanks of village streets
where moss clings for a while
in a grid of gutters
and slowly drains
the effluent of remorse
into the hearkening sea.

Then sings my soul...

RETURN TO LUSCA

Seeking salvation,
an early poet eyed her soul
and called this island Lusca –
an anagram for saint or child,
or worse, a blessed abomination,
a bolom drunk with laughter
caught in the stunning
light of early morning-after;

or she could be a soukouyan,
part beguiling deviless
part divining fire, ladjablesse
of darkened day and
fire-brightened night,
both halves chaliced in
her blighted calabash
of changing skin.

You should run, but where?
To overcome that fear
you have to turn an island inside out,
tread backwards over graves,
scour the earth for buried anecdotes,
throw salt in the wounded eye of memory
count rice grains scattered
in the crossroads of five centuries.

Who today can recall
all these recipes?

But unless you try
you will never see
but one half of her soul
from your defeated valley

with its potholed artery,
its crumpled stream.
And you can wither there
if you so choose, and never dream.

Or you could snatch salvation
from her calabash of salted skin
and seek at least an uneasy peace
on the other side of Lusca
where she is all petalled shadow
in a Sunday lane –
perhaps in Anse de Canarie.
Yes there, that spot,

right where the road banks right,
after the humming bridge
where the river comes around
offering one hand, while the other
points you down the stony street
through gothic arches
made of old sunshine
and noon's leftover breadfruit leaves,

down there beside the
salving sound of sea.
Sometimes that is
the missing half of Lusca,
which, after all your condemnation,
lingers there, sweet-talking terms
of your surrender
with the conspiring sea.

So you wait
praying to outlive
the extended truce.
It feels like staring into noonday sky –

all warmth and blindness
and salted lashes,
watering the brown eye
with new hope.

LUSCA 2

All these truncated islands
seek their other halves,
their discarded skins, divided
between hemispheres,

their mother tongues turned
to mumbled incantations
in that constant imitation
which is the backward step.

The tear of separation
burns like salt in the open wound,
making a wrong-side garment
from our cloth of seamless blue.

But who remembers?
And if they do, what then
but to duck and blink
and let the blindness pass

and hope to find that other half
of Lusca lying there inside you,
waiting at the crossroads
of your love and desperation.

Lusca, with her wrong-side foot,
her hollowed hemispheres
of salted skin, scatters the days,
holds back the hour

when doubt's fire would flare up
and consume us.
We could run, but where?
And with Lusca's eye

upon your back, how to cross
a sea blue as hope,
unfathomable as fear
fluid as wanderings?

So, who are we
to want to flee from here?

RITUALSONG

for LaBorde, late master of his drum

Such freedom is not given;
it is a journey taken, moving, empty,
aching to replant memories

and see them flowering
in dark places where the spirit stirs
and waits for incarnation.

This mas' has a meaning
deep like a bass pan in your chest,
a heaving flood of colour,

oceans of energy
washing over and around you
and brazen like a riot,

taking your feet down
through the city, on the stage
strumming to a thousand feet

feeling for song and rum
and more song, like when dance done
and it still have music

in your ears, in your groin,
beating to the steps of feet
that have made the journey

to the centre
where the secret spirit lives
and will rise again singing

singing freedom to the night
then into the light again.
Oh, to sing again

to dance again, to remember
how to sing, sing freedom,
sing freedom song…

Sing!

FIDELITIES

for Linda

When younger worlds would madden
we lie unmoored but not adrift,

breathing shallow between waves
of unworded restlessness and intermittent sighs.

We wait as August dies, knowing
truly those holidays are over,

for already October waits
to hang her harvest lamp in our high window

framing eastern hills.
Beyond that sill there is only unlit sea

which knows no season,
nor the patient work of harvest

long after love's first flowering;
nor how to lie awake

trusting our twilight,
the slow colouring of the eye,

which eases us
into these latter days,

outlasting rains, half-moons
and hurricanes of the heart.

KAWEM'S PEOPLE

They return,
ill suited, gloved and hatted country folk,
not in the hulls of SS *Colombie*
or the faithful *Federal Palm* or *Maple*,
nor by the steamship *Franca-C* of their first
crossing to Southampton.

No more travelled now
for all of thirty, maybe forty years existence,
they re-cross the void
that sailed them into vassalage
and lonely, quiet cursing under
Wilson, Heath and Thatcher.

Something finally broke
the chain of decades,
of feeling out of place at London's finest,
of homesickness at Brixton market
and living the illusion
of West-end window shopping,

of Black women being trapped
in hose ten shades too pale,
hot-press, sponge rollers, and vas'leen.
The telltale checkered grip is gone
but not the taped and bulging cardboard box,
the hallmark of their cargoes:

dasheen, banja,
macambou, zaboka;
and liniments — chandelle molle, sof' candle,
shilling oil; and spices — chichima, cannelle
cinnamon, miscade
and graisse-cacao.

They re-cross the void,
descending seven-four-sevens,
in search of Desruisseaux
and a sewette tree they used to climb
to touch the sky. They return to find
the ravine dwindled to a drain,

the crayfish sipping gramoxone,
the craggy streams of childhood
billowing blue with diathene.
Someone has built a concrete lay-by
where Ma Chopin's pomme d'amour
used to ripen summer holidays.

They recall the lyric of their language
and the taste of words sweet as tin-kwem
and zabwiko, still tugging at their hearts.
But almost everywhere Ramon's dancing violin
has been sidestepped
for dub's electric monodrone.

They recross the void
in search of Mon Repos
and Gaston's Friday-dance-hall juke box
crooning Reeves and Charley Pride.
They come in search of childhood
and go mad,

sundered from a younger generation
which settles for the drag
of its own metropole
without fathoming this hankering for home.
They build an ugly dream-house
yearning for the company of neighbours.

Then they die.
Amid good-byes the children sell
the parents' nightmare to a distant cousin.
They reboard the seven-four-sevens
returning to their own versions
of dry season.

ESPERANCE: VOX 1

February 21, 2009

Not so many suns
      even fewer seasons
since hope searched expectant sky
      for flag, freedom and
at last its own sweet voice,
      the song and seal of sacrifice
      reforming to a sense of self
      at the threshold of identity.

Yet dusk comes
so soon to find us,
      whole generations
      lingering on the edge of shadow
where no more day awaits us.

We have squandered the light
      and the land,
left the best of the harvest
in fields of idle wind
to journey without purpose.

Not even for our own sake
did we mark the road,
not with shells or river stones
nor fairytale crumbs of bread
nor even the immortelle trees
of our grandfathers' boundaries.

Where are your deeds, your affidavits,
      papier tere papa nou,
letters written from overseas –
      Brighton, Panama, Curaçao –
preserved in biscuit tins,

in the old wood safe
　　　under the mahogany four-poster?

Where are your writs and last testaments
by which sounder minds
and bodies bequeathed to you
something more than faith in death?

　　　Where are those sepia prints,
　　　winged corners and India ink,
inscriptions marking some anniversary
or Easter morning milestone,
　　　a new child's christening,
a hurried first communion
on the eve of a father's sailing,
　　　young aunts in hats
　　　and would-be husbands
　　　suited, primped and poised
　　　as famously as screen stars?

Ah, the wood-framed black and whites
posed outside the family house,
　　　tin-roof, wood balcony
　　　and modest garden
　　　shading old inequities.

What once we saved
from flood and fire
we later gave away

when the ghetto groped uphill
from the cauldron of Castries.
　　　We each took our narrow road
　　　skirting the uncouth city,
almost always north
to new continents of ambition.

Say *Nou mem ki pwan chimen nou*,
but not having marked the path before,
no swift messenger can now call us home,
no saint of light can lead us onward
to another life;

no angel painful with promise
will walk us over thresholds
bearing our mantle of dreams,
the fabric of our memories,
our crucible of expectations.

Apway an tan say vwayman an lot...

At midnight the sky will be on fire
and still there will be no light
no moonlit lore.

Tanto, Tanto.

They will take your girl-child,
your innocent,
all your love incarnate,
and like a bag of coals
cast her at the feet of djabs.

Disconsolate
for the lost way,
the clouded memory
of old habits abandoned,
the simplest rituals –
shared meals, prayers, hymns, sunrise,
the coming in and going out of doors,
intimate thoughts
and public greetings –

she will be lost,
mostly to herself
and will not wish to see
even the flutter
of the brown dove's shadow
come to earth,
nor the posturing lizard
sunning on its rock,
nor the next blossoming of forest orchids,
nor the homing sea bird at day's end,

nor you,
whose love sang her into life,
whose breath commingled
and conceived her,
you, whose every wish
will lie bagged and corded
cast down at the feet of djabs,

sackcloth of black bones
barely shifting,
black dust sifting,
fit for the making of night
which will become your chore.

You will churn it
from a mill of resignation
like a slow fuse to gunpowder,
a simmering angry dusk
settling in the soul,
dousing
deadening
darkening down.

Yes, they will take your girl-child,
your innocent, all your love incarnate,
and your first son will be among them
laying live offerings at the feet of djabs.

ESPERANCE: VOX 3

In the darkrooms
of our hearts
we turn privately
into our true selves,

then on each other and
thence from our own children.

We violate their innocence
with indecencies,
amplify the cruelty
that we have made
of compromise and infidelity.

We rob them of their dreams
too soon, too soon,
leaving so little
that is still beauty
to change the beast in us.

Cher neg passa pli wed
passay djab.

ESPERANCE: VOX 4

for Lindalu

What is this thing
you carry, under your skin,
in your head,
in this hard shell?

What is this thing
that preserves you,
hides a treasury of knowledge
and memory

like stolen bread
or holy water,
like some elixir of eternity
a force under your hand,

and in your breast
that makes you smile unseen
in the quiet night alone,
or in the shaded elbow

of the long road you travel
in your dreams,
that makes you shimmer secretly
behind those charcoal eyes,

under the beading brow
between scarred and blemished cheeks,
as if you alone possess
some ancient secret of joy?

What is this unspoken, unnamed thing
that kings and devils crave:
power to command the earth,
alter the fate of men?

What is it down there,
bone deep,
that keeps you audacious
in the face of fear

and leaves you free
despite the threat of chains,
that makes you walk toward the light
even now… even now?

What is this ponderous
wondrous thing?

ESPERANCE: VOX 5

Is it so strange
that all our hope should rest

on this lone child – yours, hers, mine?
There was a time

when they all belonged to us,
when kinship was an entire village

and nationhood a holy grail –
ultimate, elusive.

These recollections are still lodged
like so much shrapnel, rusting

in the cortex, latent in the spine,
embedded in the dormant spleen.

Meanwhile, in the dusty street
where no brave news will ever grow,

we scratch at arid surfaces
grasping for things we already know,

diving for trinkets like Prince Alfred coins
rolling off pretentious palms,

falling to a dark blue basin
hardening to asphalt.

Trinkets, coins, baubles, smiles –
they once could buy estates,

entire lives and the isles
that held them.

Now these inspiring hills,
home to our spirits,

chalice of our gentle hopes,
prisons for our too gentle souls,

hold us here to dwell like innocents
despite the devilling times.

We look upon those days
and are not humbled,

are not counselled
by how little time we took to grow;

how little time to prosper from misfortune;
how, faithful, we had hoped

to gracefully acquire a few enduring things
which, quietly passed on,

would have made us as wise
beyond our centuries, wise as we once were.

BAPTISM

Strong dougla arms akimbo,
ankles booted firmly in their silt,
she stood in the aftermath of rains,
in the angry wake of the river's havoc
defiant by her sagging hut:

Qui sa d'leau-a quitez pour nous?
La vie, Cherie!

What should God's water leave us but our lives?

Merci Bon Dieux, personne pas mort...

But houses coughed
their wet entrails
onto the aisle of street,
regurgitating linoleum,
carpet ends, bedding
and the sad school books
that would never heal –
lives displayed,
like testaments heaved out to dry
on a shelf of sidewalk
in a village where death
was a communal loss
and not the private grief of cities.

Strong dougla spirit
smiling like sunset
through day's demise,
she embraced a neighbour
with a balm of words:
Nora, you come for de funeral,
Vendredi 'ous 'rivez?
Nora, *c'est 'ous qui portez gros la plie ça la?*

Strong dougla smile full of its own humour,
she stood taller than her five feet,
taller than the defeated row of roofs
under the wide, softening sky
threatening another tide
of rum drinking in darkened doorways,
of unexpected couplings
in cool November nights
when menfolk barely linger
after sundown
for the street-lit slam of dominoes
before they turn temporarily
for home.

At the corner
by the broken bridge
two sisters tamed each other's heads;
a stoic sewing machine proclaimed itself a Singer,
its feet encrusted with mud
and memories of Ma Thom
rocking in its rhythm,
which had sent three sons through school,
raised a godchild from the country,
and married off her daughter, Grace,
the golden-apple of her eye,
to a decent man
just far enough from home.

She had made the layette
for lil' Sammy's christening,
(her first grandchile)
and pedalled through the milestones
to make his first communion clothes,
now lost in a flood of tears
with his sister Marie's little confirmation dress,
a preview to a wedding
she herself might never see.

A child, old as her Sammy might be now,
exclaimed: *Mam, look how the river
and the sea make one.*
And Mam, bitter that the one Lord
had not saved her two-room house, replied:
*Oui, Cherie, bouche la riviere ouver'
comme serpent soif.*
She cursed. Not god but his serpent's appetite.

At the crumbling waterside
of the dead-end road
an old LP of Nat King Cole
eddied in a rivulet of garments
and Brother Bob smiled up
from a floating album cover
still pleased with his greatest hits.

What memories lie silenced
in that black disc?
A moonlit kiss
near river banks in a kinder season
of lovers turned old friends
waltzing at a Christmas fête
inside the yellow-shuttered hall
that also served a Sunday school,
lovers dancing into night perfumed
with sapodilla, or vanille?
A coupling so complete,
like day surrendering
into night's sweet imperfection
in this unchanging village?

The village sobered to a snickering sun,
and everywhere people began to wash;
wash mud from their lives,
wash sacred instruments of trade,

wash away the dank musk
that hung in the street;
wash the drowned white fowl
rotting slowly at dougla feet,
in the gutter going nowhere.

And at last they cleansed themselves
in a sacred ritual,
anointing children's heads
with water from a chalice of hands,
by the river's edge,
by waterfalls along roadways
where stone facades still wept.
At last, they cleansed away
their first layers of grief.

City folks,
come to see the rivered waste,
recalled an earlier death five decades past
when fire ripped even the cotton hearts
of clouds, and rubbled walls stood defiant
like this dougla woman
in the wake of rivers,
believing in a brave baptism
for an old unchanging village.

A WOMAN IN HER HEART
for Yaz

A woman
in her heart
forsees no middle ground,
no half conception,
but will come to terms
with an uninvited truth
growing in her flesh –
inoperable,
all pain, all love.
And heaving life
into her faulted world,
will trust in the promised word
now flesh,
in the unlikely possibility
that one instant of perfection
can restore
her own imperfect world.

GORÉE ISLAND

Memory mocked us,
thrust a long lascivious tongue

through the chiselled slit
of a viewing window.

Beyond the mute stone wall
the lone passage from these vaults

made cargo out of men:
one body high

one body long
one body wide.

Still – its baleful ships
unmoored and flown –

the portal boasted only dancing light
and unblemished sea.

No voices murmuring Ibo or Asante,
just the creaking timber dock

bleached to bone by sun and salt
concealing its complicity.

BRIDGEMAKER'S SON
for Lennard

This is at best a broken bridge
reassembled in my dead father's name,

no more than a gathering of syllables
awaiting a persistent thread

to draw image unto antecedent image,
cohering the disjointed phrase,

shaping umbrage into understanding,
to move me beyond the smudge of ashes

on the corner of the wavering page,
to reconcile with his handwriting

on a cameo unframed,
his likeness in irresolute facsimile,

needing still the comfort of acceptance
so that these tokens,

these chafing remembrances
will not become

his last remains
when the real memory fades.

WHO CANNOT SLEEP

for Maria

I need to dream
but cannot sleep,
so I vow to keep
the lamp wick trimmed,
to toil while islands slumber
to oblivion,
to make these words incarnate,
make them rise like bile,
to warn that trouble walks
three steps behind
and will not hesitate
to find me
in my house.

I need to dream
but will not pretend,
do not intend
to be polite.
So I labour
with the faith of mothers
making little messages
from fragments of despair
and love,
and do not care
to abandon
such important news
on the doorsteps of
my sleeping neighbours.

These messages
will not dissipate;
they cry like nightly sirens
not to be ignored,

to be saved
from the revolving lights
which slash and burn each night
beyond the hardened boundary
of circumspect concern.

These words refuse to die.
They want to pry apart
the portal of my house,
violate my sleeping space,
question the insanity
which leaves them
disenfranchised.

Still awake,
with every instinct clenched,
because to sense
the blade of blame
scraping its sharpened steel
against a cage of bars
installed around my heart
my brain, my family,
is to doubt the sanctity
of my most precious
dreams.

And fear,
recently insubstantial,
becomes suddenly bone,
incarnate muscle,
a violence so irrepressible
that it will find a weapon
to avenge the deeds
that signed away
so many futures.

So there is nothing
but to take up arms
nothing but to defend,
to aim and gun down
this crude,
this uninvited thing,
this threatening
which dares intrude,
accusing me of treachery
in the sanctum
of my house.

Nothing,
until light comes
upon a breathless form:
my son's best friend
in whose hand
my daughter
walked to school,
who has eaten at
my mother's table
in the village
where I was born.

SNOWBIRDS

Fleeing early frost they fly
and must have surely recognised

from up on high
their own eroded landscape.

Such revelation could not possibly escape
their elevated eye:

the absence of heroic hills,
the tragic rug of alternating sage and ochre,

no brush stroke of vermillion or emerald
or accustomed deep green-blue,

just dust-grey arteries, ant-trail traffic,
recurring geometric cells,

lodging units backed against cracked yards –
a flat and uneventful tale;

no russet corrugations, no twirling footpaths
dancing up their hills;

no croton blaze or fiery immortelle,
no forest boasting bougainvillea,

only repetitious highways
hyphenating towns

becoming cities by default,
forests pried open by the prow of roads.

This indeed is a soulless Anywhere
screaming iterations: hurry home

before all that was is gone
and we are forever changed.

SANKOFA, SONG OF JÕB

for BJ

Se wo were
fi na wosan
kofa a yenkyi

His faith stands proud,
outcrop of a time abandoned,

a boulder fused from lesser stones
set in soil millennia deep.

An iguana feigning sleep
keeps the oval of the bright blue noon

steady between branch
and shimmering earth.

They all triumph here gracefully –
human, reptile, tree –

faithful as this Jõb
locked high in his yellow turban

whose offerings
of fruit and fire

also purchase heaven
for tomorrow's children.

Seeds of the Akaan tree
he plants in mindfields,

opening virgin soil
with deft and veinéd hands.

Se wo were
fi na wosan
kofa a yenkyi.

No, it is not forbidden to go fetch
what you have left behind,

but hurry. And look well, believer,
on the glorious Sankofa's tail.

Dawn is a brittle eggshell
in the mouth of the hungry soul.

COMERETTE

for our sons

1

Here at Comerette, named perhaps for birds
seeking, in watery descents,

the fossil memory of the sea,
we are nomads in a green saddle between hills,

harboured by seas, counselled by wind,
clocked by a sun burning slowly

through muslin layers of drifting sky.
Here waves beat their rhythm

against a wilderness of salt air,
sea grapes and accumulating sand

evolving into green savannas,
untamed despite the urban crawl

but corroded at the fringes,
subtly hastening our growing seasons

in a land where all horizons
flatten into blue.

2

In the haze, my children climb
the craggy mornes

pressed by the wash of salty air,
like cedars to the up-swept slopes:

a cameo of the small diluted tribe
we have become,

body language mixed by blood and history
arriving from the sea

in a land where all horizons
flatten into blue.

3

Now I pray beside the sea
to let the rush of summers slow to single frames

and trust the tribe may yet inherit
the old memories; that the urban creep

of streetlights will not banish all our spirits
to some green blackness;

that Atlantic breakers drumming
on this ochre chest of coast

will always meet the cords of cedar
on the high path over mornes;

in this land
where valleys meet the silver sea,

and horizons also rise
from flattened blue.

ENLIGHTENED TRAVELLER

for Marie-Eve

In the writing of a letter
to a daughter
journeying from home
I learn that this
has been our story
for five centuries,
this stepping in the shoes
in the path
in the shadow
in the blood
in the shroud
in the love
of those who have gone before,
and always carrying
so few possessions:
our colour
our language
some art
and our unspoken
determination.

And to my travelling child
a voice I have not heard before
but which knew me
comes through me
saying this:

Envisage first
the destination,
then the spirit,
having walked before
and dreamt of this,
will move the body
in all its raiment forward.

NAVEL STRING: 1

When we were young and poor and wise
and held each other in each other's eyes
and forced for want of means to share alike
each others' joys and miseries
we marked each birth by planting navel strings.

And lacking alternative device, erected trees,
great branching memories to bless the spot
where to more abundant life we bound ourselves,
mere shrivelling flesh proffered to eternal earth,
rock to sinew, root to bone and forever to this place.

It would have to do, this new-island soil
however small and shallow, but not without
its blessing of our blood. The rivulets of mud
at least will redden when the late rains come
to remember us to home.

For now our brave newborns meet here
in this young soil, and so will not need flinch
at death's eventual door.

You too might have had your monument
grown out, from, around and into you,
tendrils locked into your vault of flesh,

painful and deep like the love you keep
for the spiteful child of your own making.
I tell you it was possible

to truly love this place,
to be overwhelmed just by
the wholesomeness of its embrace;

to be smothered in contentment
by its green shade and offer for safekeeping
your most intimate intent.

So now imagine its green foreskin
ripped back, its leafy hand
hacked down, its earth-brown muscle

slashed to stone-white bone.
Imagine that it makes you retch –
that stench of ignorance, bile of deceit –

so that you die a little from the clog of litter
in the artery of an innocent stream.
Imagine that you die

enough to hate this dearth of wisdom,
enough to conjure floods
upon a house of fools.

Now imagine
the full reward
of a hundred labours;
your countless generations rising,
rooted like cassava
in the furrow
of your field of dreams.

Imagine music
in the flowering
of the banana,
applause from
the towering palmist,
kisses from
the red-lipped balisier.

Imagine
a noble samaan
granting green blessings
to the earth.
Imagine such a harvest
of benevolence
on your children.

NAVEL STRING: 4

But, if you just turn your face,
tilt your chin and sniff just so
even from your high green mountain
you will smell history
repeating on a western wind;

will sense the leaching from those hills
cradling your first child's navel string.
That is the scent of earth evicting us,
a whole root system
recoiling in despair.

And if you arch your spine just right,
bow your arms about your head,
tip your hip and touch your toe to the ground,
but lightly so, as if to tap the opening step
of the maroon's kutumba,

you can sense the tensing noose
of our undoing right there in your groin.
And in your dreams, where angels should abide,
yawning concrete graves await your tenancy;
winged shadows of forgetfulness

move heavy 'cross the contours of tight skin,
there on the black nipple of your child's distress
where, lacking alternative device,
she has let them touch her;
there on your mother's ruby lip

a blister from the corner
of your father's drunken fist;
there in your own protruding gut,
in your son's foreign body language,

on his putrid breath,
there is the living death
the alien seed
deep in our mortgaged soil
where faith has died
without its branching tree.

ABOUT THE AUTHOR

Adrian Augier is an award-winning artist and economist and the ANSA Caribbean Laureate for Arts and Letters, 2010.

In April 2012, he received an Honorary Doctorate from the University of the West Indies for his contribution to development and culture.

Navel String reflects both these sensibilities, exploring the human condition against a rapidly evolving Caribbean landscape, its politics and social history.

Previous collections of poetry include *Out of Darkness* (1979), *Genesis* (1980), *Of Many Voices* (1981), *Tears & Triumphs* (1982) and *BridgeMaker* (2001).

His writing appears in several anthologies including *Twenty Years of Literary Achievement* (Minvielle & Chastanet, 1998); *Roseau Valley and Other Poems* (Jubilee Trust Fund, 2003); and *Saint Lucian Literature and Theatre* (Cultural Development Foundation, 2006).

Stage productions include the folk musical *Hewanorra Story* (1997), creation myth *Troumassay* (2000), *BridgeMaker* (2001), *Anthem* (2004), *Urban Drift* (2006) and *Esperance* (2009). The stage production *Navel String* (2010) opened at the World Festival of Black Art and Culture in Dakar, Senegal.

For more information visit
www.adrianaugier.blogspot.com

OTHER ST LUCIAN WRITING FROM PEEPAL TREE

Kendel Hippolyte, *Birthright*
ISBN: 9780948833939; pp. 124; £8.99
Birthright collected all Hippolyte's earlier St Lucian published poetry, showing him as a poet who combines acute intelligence and a prophetic passion, a barbed wit and lyrical tenderness and a "a deepdown spiritual chanting rising upfull-I".

Kendel Hippolyte, *Fault Lines*
ISBN: 9781845231941; pp. 78; £9.99
With the verbal urgency of Ginsberg's *Howl*, a visionary imagination that shares company with Blake, *Fault Lines* confirms Kendel Hippolyte's reputation as one of the Caribbean's most important poets.

John Robert Lee, *Elemental: New and Selected Poems*
ISBN: 9781845230623; pp. 120; £8.99
This collection gathers thirty years of published and unpublished work from from one of the region's finest poets, too little known outside his native Saint Lucia.

Earl G. Long, *Leaves in a River*
ISBN: 9781845230081; pp. 208; £8.99
"On the morning of his fifty-eighth birthday, Charlo Pardie rose at two o'clock as usual to go and pee, but instead of returning to his bed, he left his home – and abandoned his wife – to go to the house of a prostitute." In this powerful narrative of a forbidden attraction, Long draws a vivid portrait of a rural community torn between a desire for pleasure and a fearful sense of an all-seeing and judgmental god.

Garth St Omer, *A Room on the Hill*
ISBN: 9781845230937; pp. 162; £8.99; Caribbean Modern Classics Series
John Lestrade is attempting to come to terms with the suicide of his friend Stephen and his guilt that he did nothing to prevent it… A classic novel, first published in 1968, that explores the difficulties of genuine decolonisation and the pressures of small island life.

All available from www.peepaltreepress.com